# YOU CAN FIX A COMMUNITY PROBLEM

TAKING CIVIC ACTION



Jill Keppeler

CiViCS FOR THE REAL WORLD™

Rosen Classroom™

Published in 2019 by The Rosen Publishing Group, Inc.
29 East 21st Street, New York, NY 10010



Book Design: Rachel Rising
Editor: Ryan Wolf

Photo Credits: Cover Rawpixel.com/Shutterstock.com;
p. 4 Ruslana Iurchenko/Shutterstock.com; p. 7 wavebreakmedia/Shutterstock.com;
p. 8 John Roman Images/Shutterstock.com; p. 11 Shawn Goldberg/Shutterstock.com;
p. 12 Sheila Fitzgerald/Shutterstock.com; p. 14 Dmytro Zinkevych/Shutterstock.com.

ISBN: 9781538365816
6-pack ISBN: 9781538365823

Manufactured in the United States of America

CPSIA Compliance Information: Batch #WS18RC: For Further Information contact Rosen Publishing, New York, New York at 1-800-237-9932

# CONTENTS

# WHAT CAN YOU DO?

When you notice a problem in your community, it can be hard to know what to do. You might feel like no one will listen to you because you're just a kid. It's important that people try to fix things if they can, however.

Talk to an adult you trust and ask what they think. Working together, people can fix all kinds of problems! You just need to start somewhere.

## STARTING SOMEWHERE

The adult you talk to might ask you what you think would make a community problem better. Think very carefully about this question. Even if your first idea won't work, your second or third idea might!

Once you have some ideas, you can start thinking about who can help and what you have to do. You can't **solve** every problem quickly. It might take a lot of work to do it!

POLICE OFFICER

## ASK FOR HELP

Who can help you? It depends on the community problem. If the problem is broken playground swings or a slide, you might need to go to your local government officials to ask someone to fix them. If **traffic** is too bad around your neighborhood, the police or other officials might be able to help. If it's bullying in school, you can talk to your principal or teachers. If one person says they can't help, find another person to ask!

# STRENGTH IN NUMBERS

It can help if you find other people who've noticed the same problem. You can work together! People might **ignore** one person saying there's a problem, but will they ignore ten people? Twenty people? Or more?

Work together to find ways to fix the problem and to let others know you won't back down. Don't take "no" for an answer if you believe in what you're doing. Tell people the problem needs to be solved!

I AM A GIRL
I AM STRONG
I AM SMART
I AM POWERFUL
I CAN DO
ANYTHING

Enough
is
Enough!
IT'S TIME TO
KEEP OUR KIDS SAFE!

## IT MIGHT TAKE TIME

Sometimes people can fix problems, like broken playground swings, easily. Sometimes it's a lot harder! It can take time to solve problems. Many problems aren't simple. They may have many causes. To make things better, you and other people may need to work for a long time. You may have to look at the reasons behind the problems and work to address those reasons first. Keep believing you can make a difference.

# SUCCESSES BIG AND SMALL

With lots of hard work and **cooperation**, you and other people can be successful at solving problems! With big problems, you'll probably have smaller successes before you have big ones. Step by step, as a team, you can get closer to fixing community problems. You can make sure that people are treated fairly. You can work to fix problems from traffic to bullying to safety issues. Every bit helps!

# GLOSSARY

**cooperation:** Working together.

**ignore:** To pay no attention to.

**solve:** To find a way to deal with and end a problem.

**traffic:** All of the cars and trucks moving on a certain road or in an area.

# INDEX